Stop

Ellen Catala

Illustrated by Reggie Holladay

Rigby®

A Harcourt Achieve Imprint

www.Rigby.com
1-800-531-5015

"Stop at the tree,"
said Giraffe.
Elephant did not stop.

"Stop at the park,"
said Giraffe.
Elephant did not stop.

"Stop at the house!"
said Giraffe.
Elephant did not stop.

"Stop at the school!"
said Giraffe.
Elephant did not stop.

"Stop at the library!"
said Giraffe.
Elephant did not stop.

"Stop at the store!"
said Giraffe.
Elephant did not stop.

"Stop at the cart!"
said Giraffe.

Elephant stopped!

Level B
Animal Fantasy

Literacy by Design Leveled Readers: *Stop!*

ISBN-13: 978-1-4189-3327-2
ISBN-10:   1-4189-3327-9

Printed in China
1A 2 3 4 5 6 7 8 985 13 12 11 10 09 08 07

Literacy by Design

Rigby
A Harcourt Achieve Imprint

ISBN-13:978-1-4189-3327-2   **GK**
ISBN-10:   1-4189-3327-9

9 781418 933272

90000 >

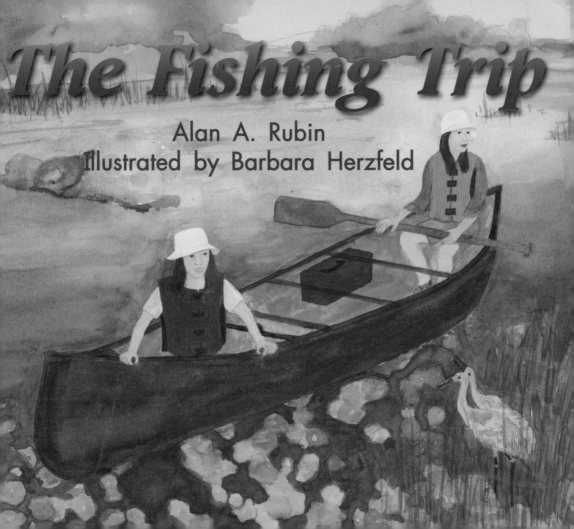

The Fishing Trip

Alan A. Rubin

Illustrated by Barbara Herzfeld

Genre: Realistic Fiction

Level 2